Michael Davitt
Land War Hero

Written by Andrew O'Connor
and illustrated by Derry Dillon

Published 2017
Poolbeg Press Ltd

123 Grange Hill, Baldoyle
Dublin 13, Ireland

A catalogue record for this book is available from the British Library.

ISBN 978 1 78199 241 8

Cover design and illustrations by Derry Dillon
Printed by GPS Colour Graphics Ltd, Alexander Road, Belfast BT6 9HP

SCOTLAND

LANCASHIRE
Haslingden

Liverpool

Chester

ENGLAND

Foxford
Straide
MAYO
Irishtown

IRELAND

DUBLIN
Dalkey

IRISH SEA

ATLANTIC
OCEAN

LONDON ·Paddington

Dartmoor

*"The **Heroes** series brings the people who took part in 1916 to life, in what may well be for many young people a first, and engaging, introduction to the founders of modern Ireland."* **Stephen Meyler**, *RTÉ Guide*

*"In its new **Heroes** series, Poolbeg Press is offering a very exciting way to enjoy history. I'm wondering, if Irish history was taught in schools through books like these, would a lot more people grasp our heritage from a much younger age?"* **Mary Malone**, *Evening Echo*

Famine and Eviction

Michael was born in 1846 in a place called Straide in County Mayo, which is in the West of Ireland. His parents, Catherine and Martin, had two children at the time, and Michael was the oldest. Sadly, little Michael did not have a chance to enjoy the beautiful countryside as Ireland was suffering terribly from the Great Famine.

At that time in Ireland most people were very poor farmers. They didn't own their own farms. They were just tenants, renting their small farms from wealthy landlords. While the landlords lived in big mansions and had very nice lives, their tenants, like Michael's family, lived in tiny cottages. Often these cottages had only one room for the whole family to live in. They survived by planting potatoes on their farms each year. The potato thrived in the Irish weather and let families have enough to eat and be able to pay the rent to their landlords. They often kept a cow for milk and chickens for eggs, as well as planting other crops like turnips. But it was the potato that they relied on most to survive.

The year before Michael was born something terrible happened. When the tenant farmers went out to dig up their potato crops they saw nearly half the harvest had failed. Blight, a plant disease, had damaged the potatoes. So there was little for the farmers and their families to eat. Also, they fell behind in paying their rent. But they hoped this would not happen again the next year.

In 1846, Catherine Davitt was nursing her baby Michael in their small cottage as her husband Martin went out to check up on the potato harvest for that year. Catherine was longing for good news, but her heart sank when she saw Martin's face as he walked slowly through the door.

He shook his head sadly and said, "It's bad, Catherine. It's worse than last year. Nearly all the crop is ruined this time."

Catherine flew into a panic. "But what will we
do? We barely had enough to eat last winter. How
will we survive this winter?"

Martin put his face into his hands and sighed.
"And how will we pay the rent and keep our home?"

That winter was one of the coldest ever with heavy snow. Michael's family suffered terribly along with their neighbours and friends as hunger grew. As there were so many small farmers in Mayo, it was one of the worst-hit places. Like so many others, the Davitts tried to survive by trying to make the little food they had last as long as possible and taking what charity they could find. But by then it had turned into a famine and people were dying of starvation. Michael saw

many horrible things in the first years of his life as desperate people tried to survive. The terrible truth was that there was actually plenty of food being produced in Ireland which was being exported to the rest of the world. But because the tenants were so poor they were not able to buy any of it. By the time the Famine was over, one million Irish people had died from hunger and another one million people had emigrated to escape poverty and death.

When Michael was four years old, he witnessed something that would change him forever. By then the Davitt family, with three more children and hardly enough to feed themselves, had fallen into a lot of arrears with their rent. Their landlord sent his agent to their farm to evict them from their home, something that was happening to millions of people in Ireland at the time.

"But we have nowhere to go!" cried Catherine as the landlord's agent and his men forced them out of their tiny home.

"It's not our fault the potato failed! Where will we go?" demanded Martin.

"Go to the workhouse!" said the agent as he locked them out of their farm.

With no choice, Martin and Catherine took Michael and their other children through the windy country roads to the nearest workhouse. Workhouses were huge frightening-looking buildings that were built by the government to give shelter to the poorest of the poor. They were cold, harsh places where people had to work hard, with little food and no comfort or support.

When the Davitts arrived at the workhouse, they were told that children over three years of age were parted from their mothers and fathers and kept separately. This meant that young Michael and his brother would be all alone in this frightening place without their parents close by to care for them.

"No!" insisted Catherine. "I won't leave them alone."

"But those are the rules!" said Martin. "They won't let us in if we don't obey."

"Then we won't go in!" said Catherine.

"But what will we do?" asked Martin.

"We'll do what thousands of others are doing and emigrate," said Catherine. "We'll go to England where we can find work."

"But how will we get to the ships?" asked Martin.

"We'll walk!" said Catherine.

England and Injury

And so Michael and his family made the long
journey by foot from the west coast of Ireland to
the east coast. They saw many frightening sights
along the way – men, women and children starving
and begging for food or lying dead in ditches. When
they reached Dublin they managed to get on a boat
which brought them to the North of England.

When Michael and his family arrived there they were shocked, as it was so different from the Irish countryside which they had only ever known. Back then, the Industrial Revolution had started in the North of England which meant the whole place was filled with mines, mills and factories making goods that were being sold throughout the British Empire and the world. This meant lots of jobs for families like Michael's but the conditions the people worked and lived in were very bad. But at least the Davitts could earn enough money to rent a small house and feed themselves. They settled in Haslingden, Lancashire, in a community of Irish emigrants like themselves. Most of Michael's new neighbours and friends had been forced to flee the Famine in Ireland after being evicted by their landlords and so Michael was brought up with a strong hatred for landlords and their cruel behaviour.

One day, when Michael was walking down the street, he asked his father, "Why is the sky here always dark and grey and not blue like at home?"

"It's because of all the black smoke from the factory chimneys, Michael – it blocks out the sun," explained Martin.

Michael went to school and was a very bright child. But back then children from poor families left school very early and had to go out and work to bring money into their homes. So when Michael was nine years old he finished school and went to work in a cotton mill which made cloth and thread. This was very hard for him as he had to work long hours with heavy machinery. Like millions of other children he was expected to work as hard as his parents. All the time Michael saw how unfair it was that the factory owners grew rich while treating their workers so cruelly, in the same way the landlords had treated their tenants back in Ireland.

One day when Michael was twelve years old he went to work in the mill like every other day. But that day a dreadful accident happened. While Michael was working the spinning machine, his arm got caught in the cogwheel. Poor Michael suffered awful pain as his arm was crushed in the machinery. He was rushed to the hospital but there was nothing the doctor could do to save his arm and they had to amputate it. To the horror of Michael and his family, he was left with only one arm. There were no workers' rights back then and no money given to people who were injured at work and so Michael was left in a terrible position. He could no longer work in the factories or mills as the heavy machinery needed two arms and hands to operate it. With little education and his family too poor to send him back to school, Michael's future looked hopeless.

But then Michael's sad story was heard by a wealthy man called John Dean. John was a member of the Methodist church, who were Christians who did a lot of good works. When John visited Michael, his heart went out to the poor lad and he wanted to do something to help.

"I'll pay for you to go back to school," he promised. "So you will be able to find work outside of a factory."

It was very unusual for a boy from Michael's background to get this chance to further his schooling, which could get him a good job in life. Michael worked hard in school, not wanting to let down his family or the man who was paying for him to be there. When he left school at the age of fifteen he had learned enough to be able to get a good job at a post office. The man who owned the post office also owned a printing firm. Michael was such a good worker that he was trained as a typesetter and bookkeeper, despite having only one arm. Michael then went to night school to educate himself further, spending a lot of the time in the library reading about Irish history and learning about Irish politics.

"I want to do something to help the Irish people," Michael said to his mother one day in the kitchen at home.

"But what could you do to help our people, son?" asked Catherine.

"I want to do something to make sure the Irish never have to suffer from a famine or be thrown out of their homes again like we were," said Michael.

"But our sort have no power to change anything," said Catherine.

"Yes, we have! I'm going to join the Irish Republican Brotherhood," Michael told her.

"Oh, son!" cried Catherine in a panic.

Irish Republican Brotherhood

The Irish Republican Brotherhood, or IRB, was a secret organisation. It had been set up to fight for Irish independence. Ireland at the time was part of the British Empire and the IRB believed that the Irish people should be in charge of their own country. Only then would their lives get better and famines never occur again. As belonging to the organisation was a crime and Michael could end up in prison, no wonder Michael's mother was so worried!

When Michael joined the IRB he quickly became a favourite of the bosses and became the Secretary for the North of England and Scotland. He was organising the smuggling of arms into Ireland, using his new job as a travelling salesman of firearms as a cover for this.

The IRB wanted Irish independence at any cost and were planning to have an armed rebellion in 1867, with help from the famous Irish-American organisation called the Fenians.

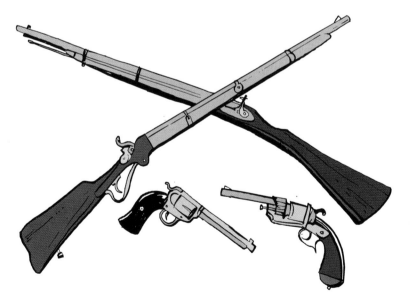

One day, his boss at the IRB took him aside and said, "Michael, we need guns and arms for the rebellion. I'm putting you in a group of men who are going to raid Chester Castle and steal the guns from there. It's a dangerous job – are you able for it?"

"Yes, sir!" answered Michael excitedly.

But the raid on Chester Castle was a failure and they didn't get any guns. Also the rebellion was crushed by the British army. The police were looking to arrest the men involved in the rebellion and Michael had to go on the run.

In 1870, Michael was waiting for another delivery of guns for the IRB in Paddington Station in London when he was caught and arrested by the British police.

Michael was put on trial.

"You have been found guilty of treason against the British Crown!" said the angry judge. "I sentence you to fifteen years in jail!"

Michael was taken away and put in Dartmoor Prison. Irish political prisoners like Michael were treated very badly in British gaols. They were kept in solitary confinement, which meant they were kept alone in their cells all the time and not allowed to talk to anybody. Michael spent seven and a half long years in a prison cell under these very harsh conditions. But in the outside world, the cruel way Michael was being treated in jail became well known and people began to campaign for him to be released. One Member of Parliament, John O'Connor Power, complained bitterly to the British government.

"This poor man, Michael Davitt, is being kept in desperate conditions!" John told the British parliament. "He did not get a fair trial or a good defence and should be freed now!"

As people in Ireland demanded Michael be released, the British government gave in and freed him, and he returned to his native Ireland to a hero's welcome.

Life was very different for Michael after that as he had become famous and many people wanted to hear him speak. He even visited America where he travelled giving lectures, organised by the Fenians.

His family had emigrated to Philadelphia and so while he was in America he could also visit his mother, sisters and the grave of his father who had sadly died by then.

The Land League

While Michael had been in prison he'd thought a lot about the lives of the small tenant farmers in Ireland which were still as bad as when he and his family had been forced to emigrate thirty years before. And, in 1879, when he returned to Ireland after the lecture tour in America, an awful thing was happening. The potato harvest had failed again! This was causing another famine. Although this famine was not as bad as the one in the 1840s when Michael was a child, it caused a lot of panic and terror among the people. Michael went to his native Mayo where again the famine was hitting hardest.

As he saw tenants being evicted from their homes and farms like his parents were before, because they couldn't pay their rent, he was determined to do something to help them.

In Irishtown in County Mayo a local priest, Canon Burke, was threatening to evict tenants for non-payment of rent. A canon is a senior priest and so this man had a lot of power. Michael organised a meeting there which thousands of people attended and they agreed that all the Canon's tenants would have a rent-strike, until he changed his ways.

The Canon got an awful shock as suddenly he had no income at all from his tenants!

"What is the meaning of this?" he demanded when his agent arrived at his house with no rent collected.

"All your tenants refuse to pay a penny until you promise not to evict any of them and give them all a rent reduction!" said the agent.

The plan worked and the priest gave in and gave all his tenants a big cut in their rents. Delighted that his plan had worked, Michael started the Mayo Land League which would continue with this plan through the rest of the county. Michael met with the important politician Charles Stewart Parnell and together they widened the Mayo organisation to the whole country and it became the Irish National Land League.

"On his own the tenant famer has no power and is at the mercy of his landlord, but if we all stand together we can force the landlords to change their cruel ways!" Michael told Parnell.

The Land League was a huge success. As Michael said, the tenants did stand together. If a tenant was evicted then no other farmer would rent the land, leaving the landlord with empty farms. If a landlord was charging too much rent, then all of his tenants would refuse to pay any rent, like they did with the priest in Mayo. When the landlord was getting no money at all from anybody he had to give in and charge a fair rent. If a local shopkeeper did business with a bad or cruel landlord then no tenants would go to that shop and so the shopkeeper would lose most of his trade! This conduct became known as boycotting and took its name from what the Land League did to a very nasty agent called Captain Charles Boycott who worked for a landlord in Mayo.

In 1880, when Boycott would not reduce rents enough for the struggling tenant farmers, they all stopped paying their rent, the local shopkeepers wouldn't serve him and even the postman refused to deliver his letters! At harvest time, Boycott could not get any men to harvest his crops.

"Where is my post? And where is my laundry?" Boycott asked his butler.

"Sorry, sir, but nobody will do business with you!" answered the butler.

This was repeated throughout the country with many landlords and agents. All this upset the British government a lot and, blaming Michael, they put him in prison again.

Politics and Fame

But the Irish people loved Michael for what he was doing for them. The Land League forced real change on the landlords and from the British government who brought in new laws to protect tenants and finally led them to be able to buy the farms they rented.

Through peaceful protest, the lives of the Irish people had been changed forever. And so they elected him a Member of Parliament in 1882, an amazing triumph for this son of a poor evicted Mayo farmer. Though, as Michael was still in prison, this stopped him from being able to do his job of representing the people.

On release from prison, he began to travel, giving lectures about human rights.

In 1886 he married an American called Mary Yore and they lived in Dalkey, County Dublin, in the "Land League Cottage" which had been given to them as a wedding present by the people of Ireland. He and Mary had five children – three sons and two daughters – and a happy home life. However, the years of being in prison and bad treatment had damaged Michael's health.

What Michael had done in Ireland with the tenant farmers became famous around the world. He continued to spend a lot of time travelling everywhere, from Russia to South America, giving lectures, and also became a famous journalist and writer. This was a time when the poor and the working class in the world wanted more rights and to be treated better. The people in other countries were amazed at what the Irish tenant farmers had achieved, and it gave them hope to change their lives for the better too.

Michael was elected to Parliament a number of times and by the time he died in 1906 he was a respected politician world-wide, a famous writer and an inspiration for many. But Ireland had lost one of its true great heroes. Twenty thousand people filed past his coffin to pay their respects. His coffin was then brought by train down to Foxford in his native Mayo and he was buried in the Abbey at Straide, where he had been born sixty years before, the son of poor tenant farmers.

The End

GLOSSARY (alphabetical order)

agent: a person who does business for another person

amputate: to cut off an arm, leg, finger or toe

arrears: money that is owed and should already have been paid

bookkeeper: a person who keeps records of the money dealings of a business

boycott: to have no dealings with a person or a business as a protest

British Empire: all the countries owned and run by Great Britain

campaign: a course of action to achieve some aim

charity: giving of help, often money, to those in need

cogwheel: a wheel with teeth on its edge, that engages with another one in a machine

confinement: the keeping of someone or something within certain limits

elected: chosen to hold public office or some other position by voting

emigrate: to leave your home country for good

export: to send things to another country for sale

famine: widespread shortage of food that leads to starvation

filed: walked past one by one

Industrial Revolution: a time in history when things started to be made by machines

inspiration: a person or thing that gives you ideas or an urge to achieve something

journalist: a person who writes articles for newspapers or magazines

landlord: a person who owns property and rents it out to others

league: a collection of people, countries, or groups that join together for some purpose

lecture tour: travelling to different places to give speeches

Member of Parliament: a person who is elected to represent the people in parliament

national: belonging to a whole country

parliament: the group of elected politicians who make laws for their country

secretary: a person who has responsibility for managing an organisation OR a person who works in someone's office, writing letters, making phone calls, and arranging meetings

spinning machine: machine that spins thread or yarn for sewing, knitting or weaving

tenant: a person who occupies land or property rented from a landlord

thrive: to grow or develop well

triumph: a great victory or achievement

typesetter: a person who sets out the alphabet on a printing machine, making words to be printed in a book or newspaper

Some Things to Talk About

1. Why did Michael and his family have to leave their farm in Mayo?
2. Do you think their landlord was cruel?
3. What caused the Great Famine in Ireland?
4. What were workhouses?
5. Why did the Davitts not go into the workhouse?
6. At what age did Michael start work? Can you imagine somebody starting work today at that age?
7. What happened to Michael when he was 12 years old?
8. How was Michael able to go back to school?
9. Where did Michael work after leaving school?
10. What secret organisation did Michael join when he was grown up?
11. Why was Michael arrested in 1870?
12. How many years in prison was Michael sentenced to?
13. Why was Michael released from prison?
14. What was happening in Ireland in 1879 that caused panic?
15. What organisation did Michael set up in Mayo?
16. Who was the important politician Michael formed the Land League with?
17. What is boycotting?
18. How did the Land League become a success?
19. What changes did the Land League bring for the small tenant farmers?
20. When did Michael die?
21. Where is Michael buried?
22. Why is Michael a hero of Ireland?

Timeline

846: Michael is born
848: Victoria crowned Queen of Great Britain and Ireland and Empress of the British Empire
850: Michael and his family are evicted from their rented farm
The Davitts emigrate to England.
855: Michael starts work, aged 9
858: At the age of 12, Michael's arm is amputated after a work accident
867: The IRB, with Fenian help, rebel against the British
870: Michael is arrested and imprisoned for smuggling guns
875: Charles Stewart Parnell becomes a Member of Parliament
879: Michael returns to Ireland after a lecture tour in America
A famine starts in Ireland
Michael organises the Irishtown meeting
The Mayo Land League is founded
The National Land League is founded
880: Boycotting begins throughout Ireland
881: Michael is imprisoned again
The Land Act gives tenant farmers rights to the land they rent
882: Michael is elected a Member of Parliament
886: Michael marries Mary Yore
901: Queen Victoria dies
Her son Edward becomes king
903: The Wyndham Act allows Irish tenant farmers to buy their farms
906: Michael dies, aged sixty, and is buried in Straide, County Mayo

43

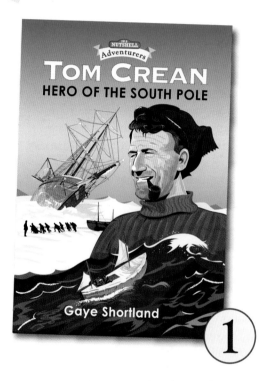

In 1918, sailors from the famous polar ship *Endurance* recorded a
ballad about one of their fellow crew members. The chorus went:

> *Hail, hail, Tom Crean, hail, hail, Tom Crean,*
> *He's the bravest man that the world's ever seen.*
> *Hail, hail, Tom Crean, hail, hail, Tom Crean,*
> *He's the Irish giant from County Kerry!*

So who was this man hailed as a hero and loved and respected so much?
Who "faced death many times and never backed down"? And how did
this farmer's son from Kerry, who ran away to join the navy at 15,
come to be such a famous Antarctic explorer?
This is his amazing story.